Prayers *with* Purpose

for Mothers

Prayers *with* Purpose

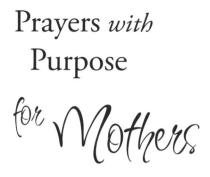

for Mothers

RACHEL QUILLIN

BARBOUR
PUBLISHING

© 2012 by Barbour Publishing, Inc.

Text selections from *Power Prayers for Mothers*,
written and compiled by Rachel Quillin, published
by Barbour Publishing, Inc.

ISBN 978-1-61626-687-5

Churches and other noncommercial interests may
reproduce portions of this book without the express
written permission of Barbour Publishing, provided
that the text does not exceed 500 words or 5 percent
of the entire book, whichever is less, and that the
text is not material quoted from another publisher.
When reproducing text from this book, include the
following credit line: "From *Prayers with Purpose
for Mothers*, published by Barbour Publishing, Inc.
Used by permission."

All scripture quotations are taken from the King
James Version of the Bible.

Published by Barbour Publishing, Inc.,
P.O. Box 719, Uhrichsville, Ohio 44683,
www.barbourbooks.com

*Our mission is to publish and distribute inspirational
products offering exceptional value and biblical
encouragement to the masses.*

Member of the
Evangelical Christian
Publishers Association

Printed in China.

*The effectual fervent prayer of a
righteous [woman] availeth much.*
JAMES 5:16

Contents

Introduction

*Continue in prayer, and watch in
the same with thanksgiving.*
COLOSSIANS 4:2

*M*otherhood! What an array of
thoughts and emotions are evoked in
that one word. One moment we tremble with joy; the next we are filled with
trepidation. Motherhood is exhilarat-
ing and exhausting. Most of all, it is a
privilege, a calling, and a responsibility
we must never take lightly.

The only way for us to be good
mothers is to first give ourselves completely over to God. Daily we must
seek His presence; only then will He
be able to truly use us. To live a fulfilling life, we must pray—for our children, our husbands, others, and even
ourselves.

My Salvation

The Power of
Unconditional Love

Don't Let the Little Ones Perish

*Even so it is not the will of your
Father which is in heaven,
that one of these little ones
should perish.*
MATTHEW 18:14

Lord, I'm so glad You often
used children in Your teachings
and emphasized the importance of
bringing them to You. Otherwise we
might fail to share Your salvation with
them. I remember how excited I was
as a small child when I gave my life to
You. When my children recognized
Your salvation was for them, my heart
sang. What a precious gift—Your love
for children.

Saved through Christ Alone

*Neither is there salvation in any other:
for there is none other name under
heaven given among men,
whereby we must be saved.*
ACTS 4:12

*L*ord Jesus, how sad You must be when You see the pride that consumes humanity. The gift of salvation was a great sacrifice for You, but now it is readily available to us. Yet so many people try to save themselves. I'm so glad You saved me, Lord. Thank You for eternal life!

Saved for Christ's Purpose

[God] hath saved us, and called us with an holy calling, not according to our works, but according to his own purpose and grace, which was given us in Christ Jesus before the world began.
2 TIMOTHY 1:9

Oh great God, before You spoke this world into existence, You had me in mind. You knew I would fail and need cleansing, and You had a plan. You gave Your Son to pay the price for my sin. I cannot fathom the depth of Your love. I've borne more than one child, and I can't imagine sacrificing any of them, but You did. How passionate Your love is!

Seek Christ Now

*Seek ye the LORD while he may
be found, call ye upon him
while he is near.*
ISAIAH 55:6

ow You long to save the lost and
dying, Lord Jesus! How eager You are
to cleanse us from our sins. From the
sweet voices of tiny children to the
final breaths of elderly grandparents,
the plea for forgiveness and salvation
fills You with delight. Oh Father, may
many more people seek You while
You may be found.

In a Looking Glass

*But we all, with open face beholding
as in a glass the glory of the Lord,
are changed into the same image
from glory to glory, even as by
the Spirit of the Lord.*
2 CORINTHIANS 3:18

You are changing me, Lord, and I'm glad. The more I see You, the more I become like You. It's a work You began when You agreed to go to the cross for my sins. To be identified with You is the utmost privilege. Oh, what a glorious day is coming when I become like You; for I will see You as You are!

Taking Up My Cross

*And he said to them all, If any man
will come after me, let him deny
himself, and take up his cross daily,
and follow me.*
LUKE 9:23

You have given me eternal life,
Jesus, and no one can take it from
me. There's nothing I can do that will
make me more or less saved. Still,
I will live for You. So many people
don't understand this commitment.
I want to be identified with You
though, precious Savior, and if
that requires being misunderstood,
mocked, or even persecuted, I am
willing.

You Brought Me Out of Bondage

And thou shalt shew thy son in that day, saying, This is done because of that which the LORD did unto me when I came forth out of Egypt.
EXODUS 13:8

Great Deliverer, I was enslaved in the worst way. Sin held me captive, and I could not break free, but in Your grace and mercy, You freed me. I want to be a living testament to the victory You won in my soul. My children need to see this. They need to understand the bondage of sin and the freedom they can have in You. My testimony will draw my children and grandchildren to You.

Work It Out

Wherefore, my beloved, as ye have always obeyed, not as in my presence only, but now much more in my absence, work out your own salvation with fear and trembling.
PHILIPPIANS 2:12

Almighty God, Your salvation ensures that I will spend eternity with You rather than in hell, but it means so much more than that. I am saved to bring glory to Your name and enjoy Your presence. You have a plan for me now that You've given this marvelous gift. I must honor and live for You. I must bring others to You.

Christ Can Save

Wherefore he is able also to save them to the uttermost that come unto God by him, seeing he ever liveth to make intercession for them.
HEBREWS 7:25

I've known a lot of bad people, Jesus. Although I must not embrace their lifestyles, I can show them Your love. It isn't my place to decide who is worthy of Your grace. I must share You with everyone I meet. Help me to be an example to my children of the truth that Your salvation is for all who come to You.

My Bible

The Power of the Living Word

As for God, his way is perfect;
the word of the LORD is tried:
he is a buckler to all them
that trust in him.
2 SAMUEL 22:31

Your way is perfect, Lord. You will never steer me wrong. When I face confusion in my life, I wonder what my next step should be, but Your Word guides me. It answers my questions about life, tells me how to handle relationships, instructs me in my role as a mother, and encourages me daily. You have truly given me all I need to succeed.

The Comfort of the Scriptures

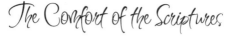

*For whatsoever things were written
aforetime were written for our learning,
that we through patience and comfort
of the scriptures might have hope.*
ROMANS 15:4

$\mathcal{L}$ord, the world is not as You
intended. You wanted us to glorify
You —to have fellowship with You.
Our twisted, sinful natures have
caused sorrow and hate, fear and
confusion. You gave Your Word so I
might learn how to have a restored
relationship with You. I don't have to
be defeated by the attitudes of this
world. Through Your Word You've
given me a better way.

Life through Christ's Name

But these are written, that ye might
believe that Jesus is the Christ,
the Son of God; and that believing ye
might have life through his name.
JOHN 20:31

We're such visual people, God.
We should be able to accept who You
are simply by faith, but You know
how our minds work. So You gave us
Your Word—a record of Your mighty
acts—to help us know and believe in
You. You looked ahead and saw what
we would need, and You provided it.

Safety in God's Word

Every word of God is pure: he is a shield
unto them that put their trust in him.
PROVERBS 30:5

Many dangers are lurking nearby,
dear God. People hate me for the
stand I take for You. Satan hurls
trials and temptations at me, but in
Your Word I find strength and safety.
I know my children are facing this
adversary as well. Remind them they
have protection in You and Your
Word.

Growing Daily

As newborn babes, desire the
sincere milk of the word,
that ye may grow thereby.
1 PETER 2:2

I stared at my newborn son, dear God, and watched him eagerly nursing. I delighted in that tiny bundle of love, and it brought great joy to see him grow—to know I'd had a part in that miracle. Father, let me desire Your Word just as my son delighted in that milk. Let it nourish and sustain me and bring continued growth.

Keeping God's Word

Blessed is he that readeth, and they that hear the words of this prophecy, and keep those things which are written therein: for the time is at hand.

REVELATION 1:3

know that my time on earth is limited and that what I do for You counts more than anything else. I've tried to instill this conviction in my children, but ultimately it is You who will show them the importance of reading and living Your Word. All I can do is set the right example. Help me to passionately study and obey Your commands.

Hearing Leads to Trusting

*So then faith cometh by hearing,
and hearing by the word of God.*
ROMANS 10:17

I want my children to trust in
You, Father, and I know You've given
me the opportunity to be directly
involved in their faith. I'm going to
share Your Word with them daily. I
commit to pray for their salvation and
surrender them to You. Being able to
take part in spreading the truths of
the Gospel is an amazing privilege.
Lord, You've done so much for me; I
want to give back to You.

My Responsibilities

The Power of a Job Well Done

Have Courage

Only be thou strong and very courageous, that thou mayest observe to do according to all the law, which Moses my servant commanded thee: turn not from it to the right hand or to the left, that thou mayest prosper withersoever thou goest.
JOSHUA 1:7

When I learned I was expecting a child, so many emotions engulfed me. I wanted the baby desperately, but I was fearful I wouldn't know how to care for him properly. But You encouraged me, Lord. "Be strong; have courage," You said. "I am with you," was Your reminder. You always have been there for me—and for my child—and You always will.

Little or Much?

For unto every one that hath shall be given, and he shall have abundance: but from him that hath not shall be taken away even that which he hath.

MATTHEW 25:29

Motherhood is a big responsibility, Father. I have to make sure my family is eating right and properly clothed. I need to keep track of all of their schedules and appointments. I must ensure that they are active in church and are being spiritually fed. You wouldn't give these tasks to me if I weren't capable of managing them. Let me prove worthy of Your trust.

Before I Was Formed

*Before I formed thee in the belly I knew
thee; and before thou camest forth out of
the womb I sanctified thee.*

JEREMIAH 1:5

$\mathcal{L}$ord, even before I was conceived,
You knew the work You had for me to
do. I'm just now learning what these
responsibilities are. I've discovered
one of my roles is to be a good
mother. You already know the plan
You have for my children as well, and
part of Your design for me is to help
mold them into people who will carry
out Your design for them.

I Want to Be Salty

Ye are the salt of the earth:
but if the salt have lost his savour,
wherewith shall it be salted?
it is thenceforth good for nothing,
but to be cast out, and to be
trodden under foot of men.
MATTHEW 5:13

ather, You use the idea of salt to remind me of my responsibility to You and to those who are lost without You. I want the world to see how good Your love tastes. Please help me to be salty!

Keeping God's Commands

And hereby we do know that we know him, if we keep his commandments.
1 JOHN 2:3

Father, my life should tell people You are important to me. I say I love You, but I need to joyfully obey You, too. I'm pleased when my son wraps his arms around my neck and proclaims his love for me, but when he does so after willingly obeying me, it just sweetens the deal. Father, I want others to see and hear that You mean much to me.

Be Prepared

And when he was at the place,
he said unto them, Pray that ye
enter not into temptation.
LUKE 22:40

It's inevitable, isn't it, Jesus? Even You had to face temptations. At least once, You spent forty days praying and facing these situations. If You needed to seek Your Father, how much more do I need to pray? Lord, I ask You to help me stand strong when temptations come, and please be with my children when they, too, must choose right from wrong.

Eating the Fruit

Say ye to the righteous, that it shall be well with him: for they shall eat the fruit of their doings.
Isaiah 3:10

I enjoy a good meal, Father, and I know my family appreciates when I take the time to prepare a nice dinner, but sometimes I fail to notice the clock and we end up eating peanut butter. That's true in other areas, too. If I fulfill the responsibilities You give me, I am blessed—and others are, too. If I neglect this work, we all suffer. Help me to be responsible.

God's Kingdom First

*But seek ye first the kingdom of God,
and his righteousness; and all these
things shall be added unto you.*
MATTHEW 6:33

I have so many responsibilities—to
You, to my husband and kids, to
my church and community—and
sometimes I get things out of order.
All of these people are so important
to me, and I want to be a blessing to
all of them. I just need to remember
that Your kingdom must come first.
If I would get that right, I wouldn't
have as much trouble taking care of
the rest.

I Will Live a Godly Life

*Denying ungodliness and worldly lusts,
we should live soberly, righteously,
and godly, in this present world.*
TITUS 2:12

Dear God, I know that if my love
for You is what it should be, all other
areas of my life will line up properly.
The world offers foolish but often
attractive temptations, and I must
consciously turn away from them;
for everything I do affects someone
else—my husband or children, my
friends or neighbors. I will choose
daily to live in a godly manner.

My Marriage

The Power of a
Helpmeet

My Beloved

*I am my beloved's,
and my beloved is mine.*
SONG OF SOLOMON 6:3

My heart is too full for words, Father. I can't fully express how blessed I am to have my husband. His love is constant; he is by my side in each situation. He laughs with me. He offers strength and encouragement. His children adore him; other people respect him. More and more, we two become one. He is truly a gift, and I thank You.

Lift Up One Another

Knowledge puffeth up,
but charity edifieth.
1 CORINTHIANS 8:1

It has been said that too often the ones we love the most are the ones we hurt the most deeply. Are we too familiar with the people in these intimate relationships that we aren't careful, or do we just expect them to love us enough to understand? Father, please forgive me for the times I've hurt my husband and children. I should lift them up and make them feel cherished. By Your grace, I will.

Am I a Good Gift?

*House and riches are the inheritance
of fathers: and a prudent wife
is from the LORD.*
PROVERBS 19:14

I know I often tend to point to
verses that pertain to a husband's
responsibilities to his wife and family,
but my focus really should be on Your
expectations of me. I know Your plan
was for me and my husband to be
joined. I was given to my husband by
You. I want to be a source of joy to
him. I want to make him glad that
You chose me to be his life partner.

Speaking the Truth in Love

But speaking the truth in love,
may [we] grow up into him in all
things, which is the head, even Christ.
EPHESIANS 4:15

Who likes to be reminded of her shortcomings? I know I don't, but sometimes I need the reminder. You don't let us get away with wrong; instead, gently through scripture and the Holy Spirit, You guide us back to the right path.

A Beautiful Adornment

A virtuous woman is a crown to her
husband: but she that maketh ashamed
is as rottenness in his bones.
PROVERBS 12:4

I have a choice. Either I can be
a beautiful crown—someone my
husband would be proud and honored
to call his wife; or I can be rotten—
a stinking cancer that will destroy
our marriage. Dear Jesus, I know
it depends on my attitude and my
relationship with You. Only You can
polish me into the shining ornament
who will be a blessing, encourage
others, and bring glory to You.

A Joyful Life

*Live joyfully with the wife
whom thou lovest.*
ECCLESIASTES 9:9

Do I make it easy for my husband
to obey Your command to live
joyfully with me, Father? There are so
many things I could do that would
fill our home with joy. Showing
love and respect for each person is
also conducive to a good home life.
Father, let us be joyful.

A Fruitful Marriage

But the fruit of the Spirit is love,
joy, peace, longsuffering, gentleness,
goodness, faith, meekness, temperance:
against such there is no law.
GALATIANS 5:22–23

When my children want a snack,
I like to give them fresh fruit. The
natural sweetness satisfies, and the
nutrients add goodness. I need
those qualities in my marriage, too,
Father, and You've provided them in a
marvelous way—through Your Holy
Spirit. As my husband and I spend
time with You, Your fruit ripens, and
the quality of our marriage improves.

My Children

The Power of the Next Generation

Obedience and Blessing

Blessed shall be the fruit of thy body,
and the fruit of thy ground,
and the fruit of thy cattle,
the increase of thy kine,
and the flocks of thy sheep.
DEUTERONOMY 28:4

Oh wise God, all that You've commanded is for a purpose. You know what is best for me and for everyone else. You've promised that if I obey You, my children will be blessed. I could not give them a greater gift! Today, because I love You and because I want Your best for my children, I rededicate myself to living according to Your Word.

The Father's Business

And he said unto them, How is it that ye sought me? wist ye not that I must be about my Father's business?
LUKE 2:49

You are truly their Father, and my children are called upon to do Your will. You've given them to me to nurture and train for a short while, but ultimately You will call them into service for You. When that time comes, help me give them to You completely, regardless of what You are asking. Help me not to fear, knowing that You are in control.

Right in God's Sight

*Josiah was eight years old when he
began to reign, and he reigned in
Jerusalem one and thirty years.
And he did that which was right in the
sight of the LORD, and walked in the
ways of David his father, and declined
neither to the right hand, nor to the left.*
2 CHRONICLES 34:1–2

When eight-year-old Josiah came
into power, Your scriptures tell us he
did what was right. I don't know who
his godly example was, but someone
had a good influence on him. Let me
be that person to my children, so that
it can be said of them that they do
what is right in Your sight.

A Grandmother's Influence

When I call to remembrance the
unfeigned faith that is in thee,
which dwelt first in thy grandmother
Lois, and thy mother Eunice;
and I am persuaded that in thee also.
2 TIMOTHY 1:5

Just how many people are in
heaven with You today because of
Lois's faith, dear God? I know it's
important to directly share my faith
with those around me, but don't let
me underestimate the power of a
positive influence on my children
and grandchildren; for they will reach
those I won't ever meet.

I Will Praise the Lord

And she conceived again,
and bare a son: and she said,
Now will I praise the LORD.
GENESIS 29:35

What a blessing it is to witness
the amazing event of a child's birth,
Lord. Of course, the blessing doesn't
stop at birth. Throughout the child's
life there are many reasons to praise
You. The opportunity to be a mother
is one of the most special gifts I have
ever enjoyed. With my whole heart,
I will praise You.

Even a Child Can Overcome Evil

Ye are of God, little children,
and have overcome them:
because greater is he that is in you,
than he that is in the world.
1 JOHN 4:4

Father, the greatest thing I can do
for my children is to introduce them
to You. When You are involved in
their lives, they can overcome evil.
In this world they will face much
negative peer pressure. Help us all to
form a solid foundation of faith, so
that when the devil attacks, they will
say, "Get behind me, Satan; my God
is greater than you."

A Heart-Wrenching Command

*And he said, Take now thy son,
thine only son Isaac, whom thou lovest,
and get thee into the land of Moriah;
and offer him there for a burnt offering
upon one of the mountains which
I will tell thee of.*
GENESIS 22:2

God, I don't know if Sarah realized what Abraham was doing that fateful day when he and Isaac left for Moriah, but surely she suspected—surely she saw in Abraham's eye that something was amiss. We all go through it at some point. We even cry for You to stop the hurt, and You quietly remind us that You make all things beautiful in Your time.

Forbid Them Not

But Jesus said, Suffer little children,
and forbid them not, to come unto me:
for of such is the kingdom of heaven.
MATTHEW 19:14

I need to take a lesson from You,
Lord. How many times do I reject
my children and their cries for
attention because I'm too busy doing
my own thing? I know I don't like to
be ignored, and neither do they. My
little ones need my love. They need to
know they are important. Please help
me to set aside my own needs, open
my arms, and let my children come
to me.

Olive Plants

Thy wife shall be as a fruitful vine by the sides of thine house: thy children like olive plants round about thy table.

PSALM 128:3

$\mathcal{L}$ord, when You compare my children to olive plants, You are making a more important point. You are reminding me of the importance of my children to my daily life. And just as olive oil was an offering to You, I must offer my children back to You to be used for Your glory.

My Home

The Power of a
Warm Welcome

Open to Ministry

*If ye have judged me to be faithful to
the Lord, come into my house,
and abide there. And she constrained us.*
ACTS 16:15

*D*ear God, the childhood
memories I have of sharing our home
with missionaries and evangelists are
clear and happy. I learned so much
from these men and women of God.
It is my desire to open my home once
again to those who are serving You. I
want my own children to experience
that blessing and to welcome those in
the ministry.

At Home with God and Family

*And Ruth said, Intreat me not to leave
thee, or to return from following after
thee: for whither thou goest, I will go;
and where thou lodgest, I will lodge:
thy people shall be my people,
and thy God my God.*
RUTH 1:16

I'm so thankful You've given
instruction and examples for how we
are to live, Lord. Ruth has inspired
me for as long as I have known her
story. She left her home and chose to
help Naomi, but more importantly,
she chose You. How very important
that choice is! You must be the
center of our home. Please be part of
everything we do.

Given to Hospitality

Distributing to the necessity of saints;
given to hospitality.
ROMANS 12:13

Showing hospitality is part of
Your perfect will, but it isn't
always perfectly easy. It's not that
I don't want people here. It's just
that sometimes I fall behind in
my domestic duties, and I'd be
embarrassed for anyone to come.
Please give me the organizational
skills I need to care for my family,
clean up after them, and still have
a home I am willing to share with
others.

Building up My House

Every wise woman buildeth her house:
but the foolish plucketh it down
with her hands.
PROVERBS 14:1

So many homes are being torn
apart these days, both emotionally
and physically. It's sad and a bit
frightening. You are a wise God. I beg
for wisdom to care for my home. Let
me uplift my husband and children. I
want love and peace to fill our home.
Protect us from heated fights and
broken glass.

Teachable Moments

*And thou shalt teach them diligently
unto thy children, and shalt talk of
them when thou sittest in thine house,
and when thou walkest by the way,
and when thou liest down,
and when thou risest up.*

DEUTERONOMY 6:7

Great Master, I have many
responsibilities to You and to my
children. My primary task is to
lovingly teach and live by the truths
found in Your Word. Each command
You've given is filled with love and
purpose. My children need to know
how to trust and please You. I
understand that for this to take place,
I must constantly be aware of the
teachable moments You give me.

Consistency in the Home

*For I have told him that I will
judge his house for ever for the
iniquity which he knoweth;
because his sons made themselves vile,
and he restrained them not.*

1 SAMUEL 3:13

God, please forgive me. I know
there are times at home when I
allow things I should not. I get busy,
and I overlook things that should
be corrected. Please grant me the
strength and patience to teach and
discipline my children consistently so
they will always please You.

Well Reported

Well reported of for good works;
if she have brought up children,
if she have lodged strangers,
if she have washed the saints' feet,
if she have relieved the afflicted,
if she have diligently followed
every good work.
1 TIMOTHY 5:10

I want to have the reputation
of devoting myself to every good
work, Father, and You've given
me clear instructions for how to
develop this reputation. I have ample
opportunities to do these things.
Make me aware when these situations
arise, and show me how to follow
through.

My Health

The Power of
a Sound Body

I Belong to God

*What? know ye not that your body is
the temple of the Holy Ghost which is in
you, which ye have of God, and ye are
not your own? For ye are bought with a
price: therefore glorify God in your body,
and in your spirit, which are God's.*
1 CORINTHIANS 6:19–20

It doesn't come as a surprise that I
don't belong to me, Lord. I am Yours,
paid for by Your precious blood.
Sometimes I forget, though. I am
Yours, and even how I care for myself
can be a reflection to others of You.

Spiritual Healing First

Bless the LORD, O my soul,
and forget not all his benefits:
who forgiveth all thine iniquities;
who healeth all thy diseases.
PSALM 103:2–3

Jesus, people come to You for physical healing, but the first thing You do is address their spiritual condition. It's not that our health is unimportant. You just want us to have our priorities straight. Lord, let me learn from Your example. My children have many needs, but the greatest of these is spiritual. I will pray for and with them, and we'll study Your Word together.

Prayer and Healing

And the prayer of faith shall save the
sick, and the Lord shall raise him up;
and if he have committed sins,
they shall be forgiven him.
JAMES 5:15

I try doctors and medication. I try
whatever this article or that relative
suggests, but real healing comes only
when I turn my condition over to
You. You just want me to pray. When
I pray for my child who is out late,
I don't worry. When I pray that my
family will escape the virus, I dole out
the best immunity. When I release
problems to You, You answer prayers.

Refreshing Music

*And it came to pass, when the evil
spirit from God was upon Saul,
that David took an harp, and played
with his hand: so Saul was refreshed,
and was well, and the evil spirit
departed from him.*
1 Samuel 16:23

I offer my praise, Lord, for the
refreshment I find in godly music. At
times I feel the chaos of the moment
will lead to my collapse. My day is
overcrowded, yet my children want
more activities. My husband's requests
are easy to meet on a normal day,
but today I feel as if my head will
explode. Thank You for beautiful
music to soothe my soul.

Wash and Be Clean

And his servants came near,
and spake unto him, and said,
My father, if the prophet had bid thee
do some great thing, wouldest thou not
have done it? how much rather then,
when he saith to thee, Wash,
and be clean?
2 KINGS 5:13

Lord, I could choose to eat
properly and exercise regularly and
get the right amount of sleep. Instead
I make excuses for ignoring these
simple solutions for better health. For
my sake and that of my family, help
me to put them into practice.

Smiles or Broken Hearts

*A merry heart maketh a cheerful
countenance: but by sorrow of
the heart the spirit is broken.*

PROVERBS 15:13

Father, sometimes my heart is so
filled with sorrow I wonder if I'll ever
smile again. I am exhausted by the
weight on my shoulders. I try to bear
it alone, and the load drags down the
corners of my mouth. But You can
put the smile back on my lips. You
can brighten my countenance. You
can restore my mind and body, and
You will when I let You.

I Shall See God

*For I know that my redeemer liveth,
and that he shall stand at the latter day
upon the earth: and though after my
skin worms destroy this body,
yet in my flesh shall I see God.*
JOB 19:25–26

I'm feeling miserable today, Lord.
The children have been sick the last
few days, and I'm not getting any
sleep. I don't have the time or desire
to eat properly, and the strain is really
catching up to me. I wonder if I'll be
able to go on. I'm thankful for the
promise that even though my body
is wearing down and will one day be
destroyed, I will still stand before You
in the flesh.

Healing Faith

*And he said unto her, Daughter,
be of good comfort: thy faith hath
made thee whole; go in peace.*
LUKE 8:48

Some physical challenges I don't
understand, oh great Physician. The
problems prevent me from being
the wife and mother I desire to be
because I'm frightened and in pain. I
am powerless to resolve the situation,
but You are not. Often the only thing
preventing healing is my lack of faith.
Forgive me, Lord, and heal me.

God Rested

And on the seventh day God ended his work which he had made; and he rested on the seventh day from all his work which he had made.

GENESIS 2:2

There is truth in the statement that a mother's work is never done. But even You took time to rest, Lord. I can't expect to do my best without taking time to sleep. It's not always easy—I'm rarely caught up. But help me to remember that if You took time out to rest, I surely can't do without it.

My Joy

The Power of
Fellowship with God

I Will Rejoice

And ye now therefore have sorrow:
but I will see you again,
and your heart shall rejoice,
and your joy no man taketh from you.
JOHN 16:22

You are with me, dear Jesus. What more could I wish? Just being with You today makes my heart sing, and it's a joy no one can steal from me. You have given it freely, and You want it to be mine. I cherish this treasure, and I want those around me to experience it, too. Let my life so exude Your joy that my husband, my children, and everyone I meet will desire You, too.

The Joy of the Lord Is My Strength

For the joy of the LORD is your strength.
NEHEMIAH 8:10

I'm tired today, dear God. There have been moments when I thought I couldn't take another step. The truth is that I can't move forward without You. But You are with me. Your yoke is easy; Your burden is light. You want to take the pressure off me. What a joy it is for me to walk with You—to draw strength from You. What a wondrous gift to be in Your company.

Sing with Gladness

*Therefore the redeemed of the LORD shall
return, and come with singing unto
Zion; and everlasting joy shall be upon
their head: they shall obtain gladness
and joy; and sorrow and mourning
shall flee away.*

ISAIAH 51:11

Blessed Redeemer, my heart is
filled with rejoicing! Death and the
grave have no claim on me, for in
You I have my victory. One day I will
leave the trials of this world behind
and enter the gates of heaven. Oh,
what a day that will be! And what
joy to know my children will join me
as we meet loved ones who've gone
before us. A great day is coming!

An Obvious Command

Rejoice evermore.
1 THESSALONIANS 5:16

"Rejoice evermore. . .if the kids clean their rooms and eat their vegetables. Rejoice evermore. . .if the electric bill doesn't increase, I don't lose my keys, and no one is ill." I'm wrong, Lord. I've no business adding to Your perfect Word. You simply said, "Rejoice evermore." Period.

Tidings of Great Joy

And the angel said unto them, Fear not:
for, behold, I bring you good tidings of
great joy, which shall be to all people.
LUKE 2:10

Dear God, when I found out
I was expecting, I couldn't wait
to share the news with everyone.
Then when the baby arrived, I was
filled with tremendous joy, and
everyone celebrated with me. Yet this
glorious event in my life can't begin
to compare with the joyful tidings
proclaimed by the angels the night
Your Son was born. It is Your Son
who makes my life worth living!

Fruit of the Spirit

*Now the God of hope fill you with
all joy and peace in believing,
that ye may abound in hope,
through the power of the Holy Ghost.*
ROMANS 15:13

I don't see how I can be Your child
and not have joy in my life, dear
God. You will cultivate joy within me
if I will let You. Then others will see
it. My family, my friends—everyone
will want You to be their gardener,
too. Please let the soil of my heart be
fertile for the seeds You want to sow.

Joy in God's Word

These things have I spoken unto you,
that my joy might remain in you,
and that your joy might be full.
JOHN 15:11

You are my guide and instructor,
dear God. Your precious Word
tells me. It provides the insight I need
to be a godly wife and to bring up my
children in a manner that pleases You.
You teach me how to serve You and
to minister to others. You've given
everything I need to live an abundant
life, and You did it so my joy would
be full. How glad I am to have a
personal God.

My Peace

The Power of
Complete Trust
in God

Perfect Peace

Thou wilt keep him in perfect peace,
whose mind is stayed on thee:
because he trusteth in thee.
ISAIAH 26:3

This is a passage I want my children
to memorize. Such a promise and a
challenge are packed into this nugget
of scripture. You want us to fill our
souls with peace in spite of the terrors
around us. If our focus is on You and
Your omnipotence, we will trust You.
You can envelop us in Your peace.
What an amazing God You are!

To Be Spiritually Minded

For to be carnally minded is death;
but to be spiritually minded
is life and peace.
ROMANS 8:6

Jesus, before You saved me, I was drawn to sinful pleasures. They left me empty. After I accepted You and began to focus on godly things, I discovered new peace. This is what I want for my children. Although only You can save them, I can surround them with purity as much as possible, and I ask You to make them spiritually minded.

The Quietness of God

When he giveth quietness,
who then can make trouble?
JOB 34:29

We witnessed an unbelievable storm last night. The first crash of thunder brought the children running. Suddenly the power ceased. Slowly the children crept to me, and I softly told the story of the time You calmed the storm. Their breathing slowed; they slept. Your peace filled our home in the midst of the storm.

Strength and Peace

The LORD will give strength
unto his people; the LORD will
bless his people with peace.
PSALM 29:11

It's interesting the way You couple
strength and peace. It almost seems
as if they don't go together. Still, I am
reminded of my husband as he plays
with our children. He's strong and
could easily hurt them, but he loves
them and keeps his strength under
control. They feel safe and loved and
at peace. That's how we feel in Your
presence, Lord.

Paths of Peace

*Her ways are ways of pleasantness,
and all her paths are peace.*
PROVERBS 3:17

All-knowing God, I realize
Proverbs 3:17 is describing wisdom,
but I would love for those words to
describe me, too. I need to be able
to handle the necessary discipline
with a calm spirit. I need to help my
children resolve their differences in
a positive way. I need to handle the
pressures of daily life with a serenity
that comes from You. Lord, make my
paths peaceable.

Perfection and Peace

Mark the perfect man,
and behold the upright:
for the end of that man is peace.
PSALM 37:37

Everyone wants to experience
peace, Lord. It's obvious that human
attempts are limited at best. But
You've made it clear that perfection
leads to peace. "Impossible," many
will say, but You aren't saying we'll
never make mistakes. You're simply
saying that if we walk according to
Your Word and sincerely grow in
faith, Your peace will result.

Getting Along

❁

If it be possible, as much as lieth in you,
live peaceably with all men.
ROMANS 12:18

I'm always trying to teach my children to work out their differences in a peaceful, positive way. I know that to reinforce these lessons, I must do my best to live them. With Your help, I will always try to work with those whose opinions differ from mine. I will try to find a suitable solution in each situation.

Peaceable Wisdom

*But the wisdom that is from above is
first pure, then peaceable, gentle,
and easy to be intreated, full of mercy
and good fruits, without partiality,
and without hypocrisy.*
JAMES 3:17

Thank You, Father that Your
wisdom is abundantly good. It brings
joy and peace to my heart, but it
extends even further. When I apply
Your wisdom to the decisions I make,
it affects my family and others around
me. It can contribute to their peace,
too. Please give me this wisdom.

The Peace of My Children

*And all thy children shall be
taught of the LORD; and great shall
be the peace of thy children.*
ISAIAH 54:13

I'm so glad You want to teach my
children, Lord. When they learn from
You, they will discover all they need
to know about the world and the
people around them. They will have
no reason to fear, for they will have
received their instruction from the
Master. I dedicate myself to helping
my children discover the lessons You
have for them so they can be at peace.

My Fears

The Power of a Sound Mind

No Fear in Love

There is no fear in love;
but perfect love casteth out fear:
because fear hath torment.
He that feareth is not made
perfect in love.
1 JOHN 4:18

Sometimes when I think of the future, I am frightened for my children. What if they turn from You, Lord? What if they become involved in sin? Then I remember that dwelling on these possibilities won't help matters. What I need to do is shower my children with godly love and spend much time praying for them. After all, they are in Your hands.

Mercy and Fear

And his mercy is on them that fear hi[m]
from generation to generation.
LUKE 1:50

I've learned that fear is a g[ood] [t]ool
if it doesn't consume me. [I kno]w You
are an awesome God. I'll [be b]lessed if
I respect You. If I take [it] [l]ightly, I'll
pay the consequence[s.]

God Fights My Battles

*Hear, O Israel, ye approach this day
unto battle against your enemies:
let not your hearts faint, fear not,
and do not tremble, neither be
ye terrified because of them;
for the LORD your God is he that
goeth with you, to fight for you
against your enemies, to save you.*

DEUTERONOMY 20:3–4

Lord, I am determined to take a stand for You. There will be those who oppose me, and I will have battles to fight. Unfortunately, there might even be times when another Christian will wish to do battle. I will not fear. It is You who will fight for me.

Depart from Evil

Be not wise in thine own eyes:
fear the LORD, and depart from evil.
PROVERBS 3:7

My arrogance gets me into trouble sometimes. I enter into situations I think I'm strong enough to handle, and I forget to seek Your direction, Father. Then I stumble. I hurt myself and others just because I don't fear You as much as I should. Instead of fleeing evil, I walk right into its path. Forgive me, Lord. Change my attitude. Help me to walk according to Your wisdom.

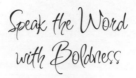

Speak the Word with Boldness

And now, Lord, behold their threatenings: and grant unto thy servants, that with all boldness they may speak thy word.
ACTS 4:29

In some areas of the world, any mention of You is forbidden, Lord. So many Christians give in to the threats. Oh Lord, grant me boldness. I want to do my part to win souls for Your kingdom. I want my children to understand Your truths, and I want them to grow up courageously proclaiming Your name.

Fast and Pray

Go. . .and fast ye for me,
and neither eat nor drink three days,
night or day: I also. . .will fast likewise;
and so will I go in unto the king,
which is not according to the law:
and if I perish, I perish.
ESTHER 4:16

God, it seems ironic that Esther's task involved risking her life in order to beg that it be spared. Many people were fasting and praying for her, and what a miracle was born! At times I, too, face fearsome duties. Rather than fleeing them, I will fast and pray and place the situation in Your hands.

Don't Anger God

*And the anger of the LORD was kindled
against Moses, and he said, Is not Aaron
the Levite thy brother? I know that he
can speak well. And also, behold,
he cometh forth to meet thee:
and when he seeth thee,
he will be glad in his heart.*

EXODUS 4:14

Most powerful God, how many
times have I caused You anger because
I was afraid to do what You told me?
Lord, I know that if You tell me to
do something, You will empower me.
Give me courage to do what's right. I
don't want to cause Your wrath, and I
don't want to miss Your blessing.

My Purpose

The Power of
Positive Influence

Glorify God

Whether therefore ye eat,
or drink, or whatsoever ye do,
do all to the glory of God.
1 CORINTHIANS 10:31

Father, my daughter's class is going on a field trip. She begged me to go as a chaperone, but I couldn't take off work to do it. I feel angry that my job sometimes prevents me from being where I want to be, but You know best. You've given me my job, and I need to honor You by doing my best. Please make my attitude right.

Created for a Purpose

For by him were all things created,
that are in heaven, and that are in
earth, visible and invisible,
whether they be thrones, or dominions,
or principalities, or powers: all things
were created by him, and for him.
COLOSSIANS 1:16

Dear Creator of all things, when You spoke this world into existence, when You formed me with Your hands, they weren't just random acts of Your power. All creation, including me, is intended to glorify and praise You. I need to convey this message to my children. They need to understand that they, too, are here to honor You. Together we can exalt Your name.

God's Instructions

*And God blessed them, and God said
unto them, Be fruitful, and multiply,
and replenish the earth, and subdue it:
and have dominion over the fish of
the sea, and over the fowl of the air,
and over every living thing that
moveth upon the earth.*

GENESIS 1:28

Lord, from the earliest days of
creation, You said You want me to
care for the earth in a way that pleases
You. You want me to bring children
into the world who also will help
care for it. I am to learn what I can
about Your creation and to help my
children understand it, for it is indeed
amazing.

A Shining Light

That ye may be blameless and harmless,
the sons of God, without rebuke,
in the midst of a crooked and
perverse nation, among whom ye
shine as lights in the world.
PHILIPPIANS 2:15

Light makes me feel good, Father. I love it when the sun comes streaming through my windows. Light offers hope. That's what I want to do. I want to draw my children to You. I want my friends and neighbors and even people I don't know to see You in me. Let me be a light for You, Father.

My Testimony

Having your conversation honest among the Gentiles: that, whereas they speak against you as evildoers, they may by your good works, which they shall behold, glorify God in the day of visitation.

1 PETER 2:12

Father, by Your grace You saved me. Salvation is a grand gift, but You don't want me to keep it to myself. You always planned for me to share it. Many people won't want it. They'll look for evidence in my life to discredit all I say. Help me to live in such a way that they won't find anything. My purpose is to draw them to You. Let my life and speech do just that.

Sleep as a Reward

The sleep of a labouring man is sweet,
whether he eat little or much:
but the abundance of the rich
will not suffer him to sleep.
ECCLESIASTES 5:12

It was a busy day, Lord, and truthfully I'm exhausted, but I feel great. What a day full of work! You intend for me to work hard. Now I know I'll get a good night's sleep.

The Results of the Rod of Reproof

The rod and reproof give wisdom:
but a child left to himself bringeth
his mother to shame.

PROVERBS 29:15

My children have big ideas, Lord.
They want to do things their own
way. Still, I know that to develop
wisdom and responsibility, they need
to be corrected while they are young.
Please give me the direction I need to
guide them into becoming properly
independent.

A Woman Who Fears the Lord

*Favour is deceitful, and beauty is vain:
but a woman that feareth the LORD,
she shall be praised.*
PROVERBS 31:30

Father, there are many material things to tempt me. At times I'm drawn to them. And society tells me that to be truly successful, I must be beautiful. I know there's nothing wrong with being attractive, but the reason You put me here is to fear and honor You. Real beauty and success lie in my desire to glorify You.

My Wages

*And in the same house remain,
eating and drinking such things as they
give: for the labourer is worthy of his
hire. Go not from house to house.*
LUKE 10:7

Father, I have the opportunity to
teach my children that You love them.
I get to be a part of their acceptance of
You. You allow me to aid them in their
spiritual growth and understanding.
As I watch them develop into young
people who honor You, I realize the
compensation of my life's work is
beyond compare.

My Finances

The Power of
Good Stewardship

Blessed Be the Name of the Lord

*Naked came I out of my mother's
womb, and naked shall I return thither:
the LORD gave, and the LORD
hath taken away; blessed be
the name of the LORD.*
JOB 1:21

Father, I am always amazed that
Job never turned his back on You.
He realized nothing was really his,
so although his losses were painful,
he was able to endure. I know that
difficulties are inevitable. You give
and take away as You see fit, and I
must bless You.

A Willing Heart

Speak unto the children of Israel,
that they bring me an offering:
of every man that giveth it willingly
with his heart ye shall take my offering.
EXODUS 25:2

Make my heart willing, Lord,
for it's the only way my gift will be
blessed. Our church has asked for
financial contributions that really
are needed. Part of me wants to hold
back so I can use the money for my
children, but I know that when I give
to Your work, my children and others
will benefit. God, please make my
giving pure.

The Question of Loans

*My son, if thou be surety for thy friend,
if thou hast stricken thy hand with a
stranger, thou art snared with the words
of thy mouth, thou art taken with
the words of thy mouth.*
PROVERBS 6:1–2

*L*ord, how I want my children
to become financially responsible
individuals. I'd like to be able to
provide the loan when possible, but I
need to know I won't regret it. I need
to be sure that the kids are mature
enough to make their payments and
that my own credit won't be ruined.
Please provide the wisdom I need.

Stir My Heart

*And they came, every one whose heart
stirred him up, and every one whom his
spirit made willing, and they brought
the LORD's offering to the work of the
tabernacle of the congregation,
and for all his service,
and for the holy garments.*
EXODUS 35:21

It's exciting to have some small part
in increasing Your kingdom, God. At
times it seems hard to let go of that
hard-earned extra bit of cash, but
what joy when I do! So stir my heart,
Father. Make me a willing giver.

More Than Enough

And they spake unto Moses, saying,
The people bring much more than
enough for the service of the work,
which the LORD commanded to make.
EXODUS 36:5

*E*verything costs so much these
days, Father. Updates, repairs,
insurance, small supplies—nothing is
free, but much is worthwhile. If You'll
do a work in our hearts, we Your
people will bring more than enough.
We'll abundantly offer our time,
talents, and finances, and we'll leave a
godly heritage for our kids.

Treasure in Heaven

*Jesus said unto him, If thou wilt be
perfect, go and sell that thou hast,
and give to the poor, and thou
shalt have treasure in heaven:
and come and follow me.*
MATTHEW 19:21

Good Master, how sad You must
have been the day the wealthy young
man turned his back on You in favor
of his riches. How often do I hurt
You by putting "things" before my
relationship with You? I don't have
great wealth, but at times my attitude
isn't much different than this man's.
Forgive me, Jesus. I want to follow
You fully.

Be Content

Let your conversation be without covetousness; and be content with such things as ye have: for he hath said, I will never leave thee, nor forsake thee.
HEBREWS 13:5

I don't understand, Lord. The people next door just built a huge addition, and they only have one child! Our small house is crowded, but we can't afford to add on. I'm tempted to complain, but then I remember that You live here with us, too. You'll never leave us, and You don't complain about tight spaces. You help us, and You let us enjoy each other in our cozy little home.

My Service

The Power of
a Willing Heart

Gladness

I was glad when they said unto me,
Let us go into the house of the LORD.
PSALM 122:1

I'm ashamed to admit I don't always feel glad about going to church, Lord. Please give me a better attitude. Restore the gladness that comes from fellowship with other believers. There is so much I can give and gain. Besides, my children need the opportunity. Lord, I will be glad.

Teaching Children to Serve

And the child did minister unto
the LORD before Eli the priest.
1 SAMUEL 2:11

As a mother of small children, I am extremely busy. There are some tasks I could be teaching my children to perform, but so often it's easier to do them myself. God, I know You are continually working on me to make me a better servant. I cannot refuse to do the same for my little ones. They might balk at it as I often do, but together we'll be works in progress.

Muddy Feet

*If I then, your Lord and Master,
have washed your feet; ye also ought
to wash one another's feet.*
JOHN 13:14

Recently we have had a good
deal of rain, and the children have
been thoroughly enjoying the mud.
As I scrubbed the mud from between
my son's toes, I thought about Your
example when You washed the
disciples' feet. I want to follow Your
lead. I want to bless my family and
others. I only ask for a servant's heart.

A Lesson from Dorcas

*Now there was at Joppa a certain
disciple named Tabitha, which by
interpretation is called Dorcas:
this woman was full of good works
and almsdeeds which she did.*

ACTS 9:36

*B*efore Dorcas died, she was loved
for her giving heart. She honored
You, and You wanted to use her
further, so You raised her from the
dead. Perhaps people heard what had
happened and were saved. I'd like to
be able to claim Philippians 1:24–25
with Dorcas and Paul. To die is to be
with Christ, but to remain on earth is
to be a blessing to others.

The Proper Attitude

But lay up for yourselves treasures in heaven, where neither moth nor rust doth corrupt, and where thieves do not break through nor steal.
MATTHEW 6:20

I need wisdom in teaching my children the proper attitude about service, God. I want them to have a healthy amount of pride in their work so they will do their best. At the same time, they need to understand that human praise pales in comparison to the joy that comes from pleasing You. It's a touchy situation. Please give me guidance.

Labor of Love

For God is not unrighteous to forget
your work and labour of love,
which ye have shewed toward his name,
in that ye have ministered to
the saints, and do minister.
HEBREWS 6:10

Sometimes it seems as if being a
mother is all labor; other times it's
all love. Usually it's a balance of the
two. In any case, it is very time-
consuming. I don't always have the
time or the energy to serve others as
I would like to, and I feel guilty. Yet
I am reminded that ministering to
my children is a high calling. You will
not overlook it, and You will bless me
when I can help others.

With Christ Living in Us

*I am crucified with Christ: nevertheless
I live; yet not I, but Christ liveth in me:
and the life which I now live in
the flesh I live by the faith of the
Son of God, who loved me,
and gave himself for me.*
GALATIANS 2:20

We've been praying hard for one
of our friends to receive You, Lord.
We share the Gospel with her, and
week after week the children invite
her to church. She's just so afraid
of what she'll have to give up if she
accepts You. Oh Lord, help her to see
what she will gain if she does allow
You to live within her. Open her eyes
so that she'll understand that living
with You truly is life.

My Faith

The Power of
Hope in God

A Reason to Believe

*Looking unto Jesus the author and
finisher of our faith; who for the joy
that was set before him endured
the cross, despising the shame,
and is set down at the right hand
of the throne of God.*

HEBREWS 12:2

You are the best example of faith
I could hope for, Lord Jesus. You
knew all that You would face, and
You went through with it anyway. All
that You've ever done or will do gives
me a reason to trust You. I can recall
many times that I've been blessed
when I've trusted in You, and I know
that one day I'll receive the ultimate
reward—eternity with You.

God Will Fight Our Battles

*With him is an arm of flesh;
but with us is the LORD our God
to help us, and to fight our battles.*
2 CHRONICLES 32:8

*D*ear God, I want to raise my children by the instructions You have given, but at times it seems I'm on the front lines of a very heated battle. This world's standards are not based on Your Word, and they make it increasingly difficult to do right. You are on my side. My confidence is in You, and You will be victorious.

Believe Only

But when Jesus heard it, he answered him, saying, Fear not: believe only, and she shall be made whole.
LUKE 8:50

"Believe Only." It sounds simple, Jesus, but this child was dead! I can't imagine how this man must have felt, but he obeyed. He allowed You to return to his home, so he must have had a certain amount of faith already. How greatly that faith must have increased as he witnessed the miraculous resurrection of his daughter.

And Thy House

*And they said, Believe on the
Lord Jesus Christ, and thou shalt
be saved, and thy house.*
ACTS 16:31

*L*ord, I want to be an example to
my children of a strong faith in You.
I've experienced much joy in my walk
with You, and that is what I want for
them. Please help them to see that
walking with You is tremendously
worthwhile.

The Great Debate

*That your faith should not stand
in the wisdom of men,
but in the power of God.*
1 CORINTHIANS 2:5

My children are young, Father, and right now they believe most of what I tell them. They accept that You created us and the rest of the world. They have confidence in Your power. The day will come all too soon when their beliefs will be challenged by "the wisdom of men." Establish their faith in You now, Lord. Help them to understand that true wisdom comes from You.

Safety

As for God, his way is perfect;
the word of the LORD is tried:
he is a buckler to all them
that trust in him.
2 SAMUEL 22:31

As the mother of boys, I don't find it unusual to step on little green plastic army guys. Generally I'm too heavy, and they suffer a fatal blow. If they'd been in their jar where they belonged, they would have survived. It reminds me of the safety I have in You. The weight of the world can deliver crushing blows, but when my trust is in You where it belongs, I am safe.

Being Fruitful

Blessed is the man that trusteth in the
LORD, and whose hope the LORD is.
For he shall be as a tree planted
by the waters, and that spreadeth
out her roots by the river.
JEREMIAH 17:7–8

It's been a dry spring so far, Lord,
and the garden is suffering as a result.
The kids have enjoyed filling their
buckets with water and distributing
it among the plants. As the struggling
plants soak up the life-giving
refreshment, I think about the way
that the lives of those who trust in
You absorb the living water and are
fruitful beyond imagination.

My Love

The Power of
a Selfless Heart

With All My Life

*And thou shalt love the LORD thy God
with all thine heart, and with all thy
soul, and with all thy might.*
DEUTERONOMY 6:5

Jehovah God, You are the creator
of all. You are above all, yet You want
a personal love relationship with me.
This truth is hard to comprehend, yet
You require my total, undivided love.
You want my entire devotion—my
heart, soul, and strength. I cannot
deny them. You, who have given
me both physical and spiritual life,
deserve only my best.

Misdirected Love

Love not the world,
neither the things that are in the world.
If any man love the world,
the love of the Father is not in him.
1 JOHN 2:15

Are my affections improper,
dear Jesus? Am I too committed to
the things of this world—my job, my
children, my hobbies? Oh, I know
these things have their proper place,
but they should come after my love
for You. Please make them clear to me
and help me to eliminate them, for I
want Your love in me.

Serving God in Love

*But take diligent heed to do the
commandment and the law,
which Moses the servant of the LORD
charged you, to love the LORD your God,
and to walk in all his ways,
and to keep his commandments.*
JOSHUA 22:5

Lord, I understand true love
involves service; that is the object
of love. At times, though, my kids
make overwhelming demands, and
I become frustrated that I can't even
sit down to a meal without their
requesting something. I have to
recognize that love involves service
and sacrifice. It's true of my love
for You, too. I must serve You 100
percent always.

Cheap Talk

*My little children, let us not love
in word, neither in tongue;
but in deed and in truth.*
1 JOHN 3:18

Father, there is no greater example
of the saying "Actions speak louder
than words" than where love is
concerned. I love my precious
children, but unfortunately, my tone
of voice or lack of attention often
conveys other messages. Forgive me,
Lord. Give me the patience to show
my kids I love them.

The Greatest Gift

For God so loved the world, that he gave his only begotten Son, that whosoever believeth in him should not perish, but have everlasting life.
JOHN 3:16

I think perhaps John 3:16 is the most famous passage in Your Word. I learned it as a child. My children have learned it, and I hope someday their kids will learn it also. For what good would the rest of Your Word be if it weren't for Your precious gift and amazing sacrifice? Although I cannot fully grasp Your love, I thank You for it.

My First Love

Nevertheless I have somewhat against thee, because thou hast left thy first love.
REVELATION 2:4

Forgive me, Lord Jesus. You have not been first place in my life as You should be. I've given too many excuses for why this might be so, but what it really comes down to is that my love has weakened. I've allowed too many things to come between us. I've been wrong, and I'm sorry. Let me be on fire for You once more. I want to return to You, my first love.

Getting the Right Order

*He that loveth father or mother more
than me is not worthy of me:
and he that loveth son or daughter
more than me is not worthy of me.*
MATTHEW 10:37

Oh Lord, I love my husband
and adore my children. It's hard
to imagine anyone or anything to
whom I'd rather devote my time, but
I need to make sure my priorities are
straight. Help me to ensure that the
time I give them doesn't take away
from what I give You. Oh, give me a
desire to make You first.

My Friends and Family

The Power of Connection

Christ First

And another of his disciples said unto him, Lord, suffer me first to go and bury my father. But Jesus said unto him, Follow me; and let the dead bury their dead.

Matthew 8:21–22

Father, I know there's nothing wrong with being dedicated to our families, but our devotion to You must be first. It's not always easy, but Your way is always right.

Good Wounds and Bad Kisses

Faithful are the wounds of a friend;
but the kisses of an enemy are deceitful.
PROVERBS 27:6

Flattery is so destructive, God. Many people are just waiting to smooth-talk my children and lead them astray. Please give them friends who are willing to offer constructive criticism if the need arises. Although it might be humbling, let them realize the wounds only hurt for a while and will make them more mature people. The enemy's poisonous kiss, however, can bring long-term trouble.

The Right Friends

My son, if sinners entice thee,
consent thou not.
PROVERBS 1:10

Oh Lord, it's hard for children
to find good friends. Please protect
my children. Give me the wisdom
to guide them in choosing friends
who please You. Please provide
opportunities for them to meet other
godly young people, and help them to
be good examples. Give them a desire
to do what's right and to run from
temptation.

No Strife

And Abram said unto Lot,
Let there be no strife, I pray thee,
between me and thee, and between
my herdmen and thy herdmen;
for we be brethren.
GENESIS 13:8

As I look around, I am saddened by the number of families who can't get along. Father, protect my family from such a breach. I know we won't always agree on everything, but help us to work out our differences humbly and lovingly. We are family. You put us together for a reason. Don't let there be strife among us.

Together

Two are better than one;
because they have a good
reward for their labour.
ECCLESIASTES 4:9

It's sad to see people cutting
themselves off from others. Although
my daughter will play with or interact
with a number of children, she's
convinced that she can have only one
friend. Unfortunately, this notion
sometimes shows up in her behavior.
Please give me patience as I work with
her. Help her to be a friend to those
around her.

Saving the Family

And the young men that were spies
went in, and brought out Rahab,
and her father, and her mother,
and her brethren, and all that she had;
and they brought out all her kindred,
and left them without the
camp of Israel.
JOSHUA 6:23

$\mathcal{L}$ord, several Bible passages reflect people's concern for their families, such as the account of Noah and the flood, or the account of the Israelites and the first Passover in Egypt. Now You want me to show the same concern. I will invite my family into the security of Your love.

The Three-Legged Race

*Can two walk together,
except they be agreed?*
AMOS 3:3

I laughed as my children
participated in a three-legged race.
Despite the significant difference
in their height, they'd insisted on
being partners. They had a blast, but
without winning results. The incident
reminded me that while choosing
ungodly friends might seem fun for
a while, it can have disastrous results.
Help me to choose friends who please
You, and as my kids are forming
friendships in their early years, help
them to remember their three-legged
race.

My Nation

The Power of
Belonging

A Nation under God

*Blessed is the nation whose God is the
LORD; and the people whom he hath
chosen for his own inheritance.*
PSALM 33:12

Thank You, God, for this great
nation. You've blessed us in countless
ways. In the beginning our hearts
were turned toward You, but we have
strayed far from You. I fear for my
children and grandchildren. I want
them to experience what it's like to be
part of a God-honoring people. Oh,
give us revival. Turn us back to You.

God Is in Control

*When he giveth quietness, who then can
make trouble? and when he hideth his
face, who then can behold him?
whether it be done against a nation,
or against a man only.*
JOB 34:29

I'm glad You're in charge, God.
We hear of many countries that want
to destroy us. They can do nothing
unless You allow it, though. I'm
grateful that You are in control and
that nothing takes You by surprise.
Sometimes I'm tempted to worry—
to take my family and run—but no
matter where I am, I know that You
make no mistakes.

Exaltation or Reproach

*Righteousness exalteth a nation:
but sin is a reproach to any people.*
PROVERBS 14:34

I have tried to teach my children
the importance of living for You.
Lord, if only more people would
realize that each individual's
righteousness contributes to that of
the whole nation. So many of us want
Your blessing, but we refuse to live
for You. Then we wonder why we
face reproach. Forgive us, Father, and
make us righteous.

The Kingdom Is the Lord's

For the kingdom is the LORD's:
and he is the governor among the nations.
PSALM 22:28

I know our government is supposedly "by the people, for the people." That sounds nice, but really it should be "by God, for God," shouldn't it, Lord? That's the only way it can really be for the people. It's like anything else. When You're in first place, everything else will fall into place. I pray more people will understand this truth so that as a nation, we will let You be in control.

Paying for Crime

*And whosoever will not do the law of
thy God, and the law of the king,
let judgment be executed speedily upon
him, whether it be unto death,
or to banishment, or to confiscation
of goods, or to imprisonment.*
EZRA 7:26

$\mathcal{L}$ord, I discipline my children
to help them understand that their
actions affect other people. As they
grow, they must follow the laws of
the community and nation, or the
consequences will be much greater
than what they face now. Father,
please make them good citizens.

God-Ordained Power

Let every soul be subject unto the higher powers. For there is no power but of God: the powers that be are ordained of God.

ROMANS 13:1

What's good for me is good for me; what's good for you is fine for you"—this attitude seems to be a growing trend. You've given us higher authorities for a reason, though. Without parents, teachers, bosses, and government, and especially without You, chaos would reign. We might not always like established rules, but we still need to obey them.

Thank You for Our Leaders

*I exhort therefore, that, first of all,
supplications, prayers, intercessions,
and giving of thanks, be made for
all men; for kings, and for all that
are in authority; that we may lead
a quiet and peaceable life in
all godliness and honesty.*
1 TIMOTHY 2:1–2

God, managing this nation is not
a job I would want—managing
my household involves enough
challenges! I'm thankful for those
who are willing to dedicate their time
and effort to govern the people of this
land. I ask that You would help these
men and women make wise choices.
Help them also to remember that
this nation was founded on biblical
principles.

My Praise

The Power of an
Overflowing Heart

Creation Will Praise God

*Sing, O heavens; and be joyful,
O earth; and break forth into singing,
O mountains: for the LORD hath
comforted his people, and will have
mercy upon his afflicted.*
ISAIAH 49:13

I was made to praise You and Your
great majesty, oh God. In fact, all
creation—the heavens, the earth,
the mountains—all Your works
declare Your glory. Yet even in Your
greatness You take time to offer
comfort to Your people. Even with
our imperfections You have mercy on
us. You truly are a great God, worthy
of infinitely more honor than I am
capable of bestowing upon You.

A Chosen Generation

But ye are a chosen generation,
a royal priesthood, an holy nation,
a peculiar people; that ye should
shew forth the praises of him who
hath called you out of darkness
into his marvellous light.
1 PETER 2:9

Each new generation has so much to offer, Lord. I'll never forget the moment our first son was born. There was so much we wanted for our tiny son, but our greatest desire was that he would one day become part of Your chosen generation—that he would sing Your praises. Lord, the day of his second birth was even more spectacular than that of his first!

In Him Is Victory

I will call on the LORD,
who is worthy to be praised:
so shall I be saved from mine enemies.
2 SAMUEL 22:4

Lord, You are worthy of all my
adoration. I'm amazed at how much
I am blessed when I praise You.
When I'm glorifying You, I feel Your
strength. I know You are with me
in a special way. I want my entire
existence to be centered on You, for
You are awesome. Without You, my
life would lie in shattered ruins, but
You give me victory.

Walking with God

*The fear of the LORD is the beginning
of wisdom: a good understanding have
all they that do his commandments:
his praise endureth for ever.*
PSALM 111:10

Father, I've tried to teach my
children that there is good fear
and bad fear. Please help them to
understand that fearing You is the
first step in walking with You. As
their respect for You grows, they will
want to know more about You and
will choose to obey You. As they obey
You, they will get to know You and
adore You more fully. They will begin
to praise You fervently.

The Marriage of the Lamb

And I saw an angel standing in the sun;
and he cried with a loud voice,
saying to all the fowls that fly in
the midst of heaven, Come and
gather yourselves together unto the
supper of the great God.
REVELATION 19:17

*E*ven the joy of my own wedding
day can't compare to the rejoicing
that will take place the day You and
Your bride are joined, Lord. I look
forward to rejoicing with so many
others the day that celebration takes
place. I only ask that my children and
loved ones will be there to join in on
that glorious day.

All Ye People

And again, Praise the Lord,
all ye Gentiles; and laud him,
all ye people.
ROMANS 15:11

Thank You, Lord, that all people are
important to You. Thank You that even
I am instructed to praise You. You've
done so much for me every day of my
life. You give me strength and breath.
You meet all my needs abundantly.
You've blessed me with a beautiful
family. The list goes on and on and is
topped by the gift of Your precious Son.
I cannot help but praise You.

Meaningful Routine

And to stand every morning
to thank and praise the LORD,
and likewise at even.
1 CHRONICLES 23:30

All the books on child-rearing say how important it is to establish routines for children. It makes sense. You must have known we would need order, because You've told us what to include in our daily routine. Each morning we need to begin by praising You. We're also to end the day by praising You. Doing so helps us to recall Your blessings and greatness. Praising You gives us the right perspective.

My Fulfillment

The Power of
Completion

Righteous Children

The father of the righteous shall greatly rejoice: and he that begetteth a wise child shall have joy of him. Thy father and thy mother shall be glad.
Proverbs 23:24–25

Dear God, from the moment my first child was conceived, my greatest calling has been to bring up my children in the nurture and admonition of You. As each of my children calls on You for salvation, part of my life's work is fulfilled. I am hoping to hear, "Well done," one day, and I also anticipate standing with my children as they hear those words.

Why Am I Here?

*And who knoweth whether
thou art come to the kingdom
for such a time as this?*
ESTHER 4:14

Father, I can think of a few women
in the Bible who knew what You
had planned for their children, but
that's not usually the case. I think
of Nancy Lincoln and of D. L.
Moody's mother. They probably had
no idea how their sons would affect
this nation. I don't know what You
have planned for my children, either,
but You have chosen me to be their
mother and to prepare them to help
make a difference—small or great.

My Vocation

*I therefore, the prisoner of the Lord,
beseech you that ye walk worthy of the
vocation wherewith ye are called.*
EPHESIANS 4:1

I've tried many career paths, Father,
and I have enjoyed most of them, but
not one compares to being a mother.
It seems the more I invest in my
children, the more I am rewarded. It's
especially true spiritually speaking,
and I know that walking with You
and teaching my kids to do the same
is my highest calling. Lord, help us all
to walk worthily of the calling You've
given us.

What Is Success?

*Because thou hast forgotten the God
of thy salvation. . .in the day shalt
thou make thy plant to grow,
and in the morning shalt thou make
thy seed to flourish: but the harvest
shall be a heap in the day of grief
and of desperate sorrow.*
ISAIAH 17:10–11

$\mathcal{L}$ord, please help me to remember
that true success lies in pleasing You.
It's not that I don't want my family to
dress well or have nice things. I enjoy
being able to go to fun places with
my husband and children, but help
me never to sacrifice my relationship
with You to do these things. I would
rather please You than be a worldly
success.

Finishing the Job

As the LORD commanded Moses
his servant, so did Moses command
Joshua, and so did Joshua;
he left nothing undone of all that
the LORD commanded Moses.

JOSHUA 11:15

It's hard for children to grasp the concept of completing a task well. If the toys are off the floor, the cleanup is suitable (even if they're in a pile on the bed). They don't understand how rewarding it is to finish the job. I know I must set the example with each job You give me. Each day that You help me complete my work, I feel useful and fulfilled.

Christ in Me

*I am crucified with Christ: nevertheless
I live; yet not I, but Christ liveth in me:
and the life which I now live in
the flesh I live by the faith of the
Son of God, who loved me,
and gave himself for me.*
GALATIANS 2:20

Recently I was sharing Your love with a young mother who has been through trials, and she seemed fascinated by what I said. But, Lord, she has some things she just doesn't want to give up. I told her if she accepted You, You'd replace those negative things and help her to become a new person. She's close, Lord, but she's just not sure. Open her heart and help her see how fulfilling life will be with You.

A Great Compliment

Then Paul answered, What mean ye
to weep and to break mine heart?
for I am ready not to be bound only,
but also to die at Jerusalem for the
name of the Lord Jesus.
ACTS 21:13

I don't think Paul really had a
death wish, although he was looking
forward to being with Jesus. It's
just that he recognized that to die
because of his testimony would be
a compliment of the highest kind.
I've thought about that, and I've
wondered what would happen to my
kids if I were gone. I know You'd take
care of them. So, Lord, let me live
completely for You, no matter what
the cost.

My History

The Power of
Experience

Don't You Remember?

Do ye not yet understand,
neither remember the five loaves of
the five thousand, and how many
baskets ye took up?
MATTHEW 16:9

You will always provide for the needs of my family, but sometimes I don't live like I believe it. How quickly I forget that You've always cared for me in the past. I still worry about how the bills will be paid and how we'll manage all the "extras" that creep up. Forgive me, Lord. Help me to remember Your goodness and provision.

Moving beyond the Past

*Therefore remove sorrow from thy heart,
and put away evil from thy flesh:
for childhood and youth are vanity.*
ECCLESIASTES 11:10

There are times, Father, when
I am tempted to blame current
situations on the past. I realize that
what happens in our early years
can be instrumental in forming the
people we eventually become, but
that doesn't give us excuses. You have
power that is greater than my history,
and You can help me to move beyond
my circumstances to become the
woman You've designed me to be.

I Was Blind but Now I See

He answered and said,
Whether he be a sinner or no,
I know not: one thing I know,
that, whereas I was blind, now I see.
JOHN 9:25

Your power is amazing; Your love is astonishing, dear God. You altered the lives of these people so significantly that it was as though their pasts never existed. You did that for me, too. Sin had blinded and crippled me, but You saved me from that wretched state and gave me new life. Thank You!

Used for Good

But as for you, ye thought evil against
me; but God meant it unto good,
to bring to pass, as it is this day,
to save much people alive.
GENESIS 50:20

I've made some mistakes, God.
I can't change them. Sometimes it
seems they might control me, but
I want to be controlled by You.
Although I'm not happy about some
of the choices I've made, I know You
can turn them around and use them
in a positive way. Lord, let this be the
case.

Growing Up

❀

When I was a child, I spake as a child,
I understood as a child, I thought as a
child: but when I became a man,
I put away childish things.
1 CORINTHIANS 13:11

When my children first started
talking, I loved to hear their babyish
chatter. As their speech advanced,
I was happy for their complex sen-
tences and proud of their expanding
vocabulary. I know You want me
to grow, too, Lord. You want me to
move from the past to being more
like You, and with Your help I will.

My Future

The Power of Optimism

Wings as Eagles

*But they that wait upon the Lord shall
renew their strength; they shall mount
up with wings as eagles; they shall run,
and not be weary; and they shall walk,
and not faint.*

ISAIAH 40:31

I've never seen a bald eagle in the
wild, but I think someday I might
because they've made an amazing
comeback. There are times when I feel
I need a recovery program, too, dear
Jesus. I am burdened down by the
cares of this world, but I am trying to
wait patiently. I know one day when
the time is right, You'll give me wings
like an eagle, and I'll soar to new
heights.

For the Sake of the Elect

*For then shall be great tribulation,
such as was not since the beginning
of the world to this time, no,
nor ever shall be. And except those days
should be shortened, there should no
flesh be saved: but for the elect's sake
those days shall be shortened.*
MATTHEW 24:21–22

Dear God, I love being a mother, but at times it nearly rips my heart out. I fear this world my children are growing up in, and I know it's only getting worse. As Christians we will find it more and more difficult to do what You've called us to do, but we know this time is temporary. Soon You will call us out of this mess into perfect eternity.

Dreams and God

For in the multitude of dreams and many words there are also divers vanities: but fear thou God.
ECCLESIASTES 5:7

As a child I can remember planning what I would be when I grew up. Oh, the list that I went through! Now it's fun to hear my children's thoughts and plans. I pray, dear God, that they would be sure to actively include You in their decisions. You have a perfect plan for each of them. Give them wisdom to understand that when You play the most significant role in the choices they make, that is when they'll be blessed.

Seeing Christ

Yet a little while, and the world
seeth me no more; but ye see me:
because I live, ye shall live also.
JOHN 14:19

What a promise, Lord! It must
have been hard for the disciples when
they realized You were leaving them
physically. I know how hard it was
for me when my best friend moved
thousands of miles away. I look
forward to seeing her every few years,
but it can't compare to the exhilaration
of knowing that one day I will see You.
Because You live, I live, too.

Secret Things and Revealed Things

The secret things belong unto the LORD our God: but those things which are revealed belong unto us and to our children for ever, that we may do all the words of this law.

DEUTERONOMY 29:29

I know there are things You don't reveal to me about my future, dear God. I'm thankful for that. I'd likely be terrified if I could see everything. There are many things You *have* shown me, though, so I will better serve and obey You and so my children will do likewise. Lord, let me please You all my days.

A Mystery

Behold, I shew you a mystery;
we shall not all sleep,
but we shall all be changed.
1 CORINTHIANS 15:51

Oh, how I laughed the first time
I saw this verse hanging above the
changing table in the church nursery.
It was just the humor this sleep-
deprived mother needed. But, God,
there is so much promise in this
simple passage. As a believer, I have
the hope that one day when life on
earth ends, I will begin a new life in
heaven and will be transformed into
the image of Christ I'm meant to be.

The End Is Near

And ye shall be hated of all men for my name's sake: but he that shall endure unto the end, the same shall be saved.
MARK 13:13

It sounds frightening, dear God. I know Satan is hard at work trying to discourage Christians and to keep us from serving You. Give us courage as we face the end-time challenges. Fill us with joy as we recognize we will soon see You face-to-face.

Changing Address

*Then we which are alive and remain
shall be caught up together with
them in the clouds, to meet the Lord
in the air: and so shall we ever be
with the Lord.*

1 Thessalonians 4:17

As believers, we never actually
die; we just change addresses—
dwelling eternally with You in heaven.
I'm looking forward to that day. I've
only changed my address once in my
life. After hearing so many "moving
day" horror stories, I'm thankful and
glad that when I get to heaven, it will
be forever.

A Matter to Ponder

*Keeping mercy for thousands,
forgiving iniquity and transgression
and sin, and that will by no means
clear the guilty; visiting the iniquity of
the fathers upon the children, and upon
the children's children, unto the third
and to the fourth generation.*
EXODUS 34:7

I know my children will choose
their own paths, Lord. But the
example I set will play a great role.
Help me never to take my legacy
lightly.

I Will Be with Thee

And he said,
Certainly I will be with thee.
EXODUS 3:12

*E*ach day holds something new,
Father, and I don't always know
what it will be. There are times when
things have to be done, but one of
the children wakes up with a fever or
maybe I've misplaced my car keys.
Sometimes I feel so overwhelmed that
I don't want to know what lies ahead
of me for the day or week. But You've
promised that You will be with me—
today and always.

Conclusion

*For our gospel came not unto you in
word only, but also in power,
and in the Holy Ghost,
and in much assurance.*
1 THESSALONIANS 1:5

God is powerful. His answers to
prayer offer abundant power, but we
must pray. It will take a bit of extra
effort as a busy mom, but it will be
worth it for a life and a home filled
with the power of God. The moments
invested with God are the most
important moments you'll spend. As
more of us let God work within us as
individuals, the more positive changes
we will see in our communities and
nation. Let Him start with you.
Choose a time, place, and method for
prayer and Bible reading. Stick with
it, and continue to experience God's
power in your life.